ENCORE

Embracing Your Retirement Journey and Living Your Best Life

CHARLES L. JONES
BOBBIE J. JONES

Encore: Embracing Your Retirement Journey and Living Your Best Life

Published by StoryBuilders Press

Paperback: 978-1-954521-24-7
Ebook: 978-1-954521-23-0

This book is dedicated to anyone in Stage 5 (Exit) of the Career Life Cycle, on the cusp of the next chapter in their journey. We also dedicate this book to those who are in the daily grind, chasing their dreams and aspirations. May these pages offer guidance and inspiration as you embrace the endless possibilities of your retirement years. May your days be filled with warmth of the sun, the embrace of loved ones, and the opportunity to live your best life in the Encore stage!

TABLE OF CONTENTS

INTRODUCTION

Elvis Presley once said, "You only pass through this life once; you don't come back for an encore." True enough, but I have come to realize that in life, if we plan and prepare well, an encore opportunity may be *exactly* what we get after retirement. In fact, it's where I find myself now, five years after leaving my thirty-plus-year career in Corporate America.

In my book, *The Career Life Cycle: Navigating the 5 Stages of Work Success*, I identify and explore the five stages of every career: Exploration, Establishment, Elevation, Enrichment, and Exit. During each stage of that Career Life Cycle, we must pay special attention to our Family, Faith, Finances, Fears, and Friction in order to integrate work and life as seamlessly as possible. I call this the Life Fulfillment Framework.

In the past few years since I retired, I have come to learn that if you prepare well before you Exit, you can set yourself up for a rich and fulfilling post-Exit life, one that truly feels like an Encore. In the pages to come, I will share what I have learned about this new (and final) stage of our life, the Encore stage, and how the Life Fulfillment Framework informs this stage just as relevantly as it does the five earlier stages of our career life.

As a special bonus, my wife Bobbie is the co-author of this book. Whereas during my Career Life Cycle, I spent far more time away from home than at home, in this Encore stage, the tables have turned, and I'm home with Bobbie most of the time. It will probably come as no surprise that this sudden dramatic increase in "togetherness" has presented its own unique set of challenges. The best way I know of to give a complete picture of those challenges (and the gifts, of course!) is to include Bobbie's perspective. Together, we will delve into the joys and challenges of this new phase of our life and how we are navigating them as a team.

In this book, our goal is to provide readers with a roadmap for navigating the Encore stage of life within the context of the Life Fulfillment Framework. Whether you are someone who has recently retired or are planning for your post-career life, we hope that the lessons and experiences we share in these pages will help you make the most of this exciting new chapter and equip you with the tools and mindset you need to thrive in this new phase of your life.

CHAPTER ONE

FAMILY DYNAMICS

Retirement brought about a sudden and profound shift in my daily routine, as though someone had pulled the rug out from under me. From the age of twenty-one, until I retired at fifty-three, I only knew life in the fast lane. It was all about long hours of hard work with the goal of career advancement. And the day I retired, everything stopped. I found myself faced with a new, uncertain reality.

Although I was prepared financially for my retirement, it still was jarring because the change was so sudden. After the initial feeling of freedom at being able to sleep in a little bit and play golf whenever I wanted to, a sense of malaise started to set in. The sudden loss of a structured routine and a sense of purpose, along with the loss of social connections that were previously tied to my work, started to have an effect.

What I call malaise, Bobbie was concerned might be slipping into depression.

Bobbie's Take:

Charles's retirement had a profound impact on our family. We had discussed retirement at great length in the past, and he had a plan—he wanted to start a business. However, when retirement actually came, the uncertainty of it all hit my husband hard. He found himself grappling with questions like, *What's next? Is this the end? What is my purpose now?* His mental struggles manifested in waves of emotions—he'd have good days and then some not-so-good days where he'd withdraw and doubt himself.

Retirement, as we quickly realized, isn't just a change for the retiree—it impacts the whole family. We had to accept that Charles wouldn't be leaving for work anymore and that we'd have him around all the time. This shift had a significant impact on the dynamics of our household. As his spouse, I had to navigate through his emotional ups and downs and be there for him every step of the way.

Our daughters, who are now adults and old enough to understand what's going on, have also been affected by their father's retirement. It's important for us to be honest with them and not sugarcoat the reality of it all. We've found that knowledge is power, and we want to prepare them for what's to come. I've shared my own experiences and stories with them, so they know that it's okay to struggle with retirement and that there is a light at the end of the tunnel. By being open and honest with our children, we hope to help them prepare for their own retirement someday.

Your Encore:

How can you maintain a sense of purpose and structure in your life after retirement, and what steps can you take to establish new routines and social connections outside of work?

Redefining Your Role

As a husband and father, I have always felt that my primary purpose was to protect and provide for my family. But after retiring, I found myself faced with a new challenge—what was my role now that I had stopped providing? For years, I had sacrificed my time, energy, and everything else for the well-being of my family, and now that I was no longer working, I wondered how I could remain relevant to them.

However, two years into retirement, I have come to a realization—I am still a provider for my family, but in a different way. My Encore performance is about providing something far more valuable than money—wisdom and guidance. While I may not be the breadwinner anymore, I am still a husband and father, and now I can be there for my family in a whole new way. I want to be an example to them and to others, to show them what's possible, and to inspire them to pursue their dreams and passions.

Without distractions from Corporate America, I can fully focus on supporting my family and being a source of wisdom for them. I reassure them that they don't have to worry, and that I am here to help them navigate whatever challenges they may face. This is my new purpose, and it drives me to be the best husband and father I can be, even in retirement.

One way I provide support is by being present in their lives, both physically and emotionally. I make it a priority to spend quality time with my wife and my daughters (mostly calling my daughters by phone, as they both live about 700 miles away), listening to their concerns and offering advice when needed. I have leveraged my years of experience and knowledge to offer guidance to my daughters as they pursue their own careers and life goals. I want to be a sounding board for them, helping them to make informed decisions and avoid any pitfalls that I may have experienced in my own career. I want them to know they can always count on me for support, no matter what.

Most importantly, I want to be a positive influence in their lives, a source of inspiration and motivation. Retirement has given me the freedom to pursue new passions and interests, and I hope that by pursuing my own goals, I can inspire my family to do the same.

Bobbie's Take:

Although I have an amazing relationship with our daughters and give them great advice, I encourage them to seek out different points of view from their dad. Charles has always been a source of wisdom and guidance for our daughters, and even as they have grown into successful professionals, they still turn to their daddy for advice. Whether they are facing a major life decision or simply seeking a listening ear, Charles is always there to offer his support and wisdom.

Tiffany and Eryka know that they can rely on Charles for honest and insightful feedback, and they appreciate the unique perspective he brings to every situation. They also know that he truly cares about their well-being and wants to see them thrive in all aspects of their lives.

The girls cherish their relationship with their dad and seek out his guidance and support. They affectionately refer to themselves as "Charlie's Angels," a nod to their daddy's unwavering love and support throughout their lives.

Your Encore:

How can you redefine your role as a provider for your family in your Encore stage to continue to be a positive influence in their lives?

Communication and Family Dynamics

Effective communication is essential to maintaining strong relationships, especially in marriage and family life. As Confucius once said, "Words are the voice of the heart," and it is through communication that we express our love and understanding for one another.

Prior to retirement, my focus was entirely on my career, with little time or energy left for anything else. Although providing for my family was always a top priority, I was rarely present in their lives and oftentimes failed to connect with my wife on a deep level.

Even when I was at home, my mind was often consumed with work-related thoughts and being strategic. Looking back, I realize that I didn't communicate my love and affection for my family as effectively as I could have. I didn't actively listen to them and instead listened to respond. I regret not making more of an effort to understand my wife and daughters, especially when they came to me with concerns or needs.

One of the best tools to help me become a better communicator has been counseling. It turns out that a counselor or therapist can help identify patterns of communication that may be causing misunderstandings or conflicts within the marriage or family, and can provide guidance on how to address them. In my case, counseling has been particularly helpful for learning how to communicate well while at the same time navigating the new stressors of life as a retired person and adjusting to my new roles and routines.

Bobbie's Take:

As someone who has experienced the sudden and profound shift that comes with a spouse's retirement, I strongly believe that counseling or therapy should be an integral part of every retirement package.

When my husband and I were preparing for retirement, we focused mostly on financial planning, overlooking the emotional and psychological impact that such a major life change can have. Looking back, I realize now that we should have taken the time to seek professional counseling to help us navigate the transition and anticipate the changes that it would bring to our relationship and our lives.

Retirement can be a time of great joy and fulfillment, but it can also be a time of uncertainty, loss, and even grief. Counseling can help retirees and their families adjust to the new reality, explore new roles and identities, and cope with the loss of structure, routine, and social connections that work often provides. It can also help couples strengthen their communication and intimacy, work through any conflicts or differences that arise, and build a new shared vision for their future.

Your Encore:

What are some common communication patterns or habits that you have noticed in your family relationships, and how can you work to improve them as you transition into retirement and the Encore stage?

Extended Family Concerns

As you move into the Encore stage of your life, you may find yourself facing the new responsibility and challenge of caring for aging parents. My mom and dad are living happily in the home where I grew up in Mississippi. In fact, that's where most of our family is, while I'm a long way across the country from them in the Chicago area.

My parents are the type of parents who are not going to go to a retirement home. They want to stay in their house and have the freedom to do whatever they want to do. That's how they think, and that's how they were taught. I saw my mom move in with my grandma because my grandma refused to go to an assisted living facility or relocate. So that's how our family is.

As you enter the Encore stage of your life, you may have envisioned a time of leisure, travel, and pursuing new hobbies. In reality, you may feel a sense of duty or obligation to care for your parents and loved ones, but it can also be overwhelming and stressful to balance their needs with your own. You may have conflicting feelings of love, gratitude, and responsibility towards your parents, while also experiencing stress, exhaustion, and guilt. It's important to acknowledge the challenges of caregiving and to seek support and resources to help you navigate this stage of life with compassion, grace, and resilience.

If you have siblings, it's good to plan together for how to assume this responsibility. My older brother and his wife live near my parents, and they regularly check in on them to make sure everything's okay. Fortunately, they have no serious medical issues now, but we can tell they're slowing down. Not long ago, my brother told me, "Hey brother, our parents are getting older, you need to come home more."

So I do now. I spend time with my mom and dad when I can, not only to take care of them, but also to allow them to enrich me with the wisdom they have earned through the years.

Bobbie's Take:

Retirement offers the luxury of extended travel and staying in one place for as long as needed, which can be a major advantage when caring for loved ones. Charles and I can now choose to extend our stay in Mississippi without the pressure of having to rush back to work.

This is in stark contrast to when my dad was ill and Charles was still working, making it difficult for me to be with my dad as I had to fly back and forth to take care of him. With retirement, we now have the freedom and flexibility to care for our aging parents without the added stress of juggling work responsibilities.

Your Encore:

What are some ways that you can balance your own needs and responsibilities with the demands of caregiving for aging parents?

A Final Family Thought

Now that I have reached the Encore stage of my life, my priorities have shifted from personal pursuits to a focus on my family. My primary goal is to give them my full attention and support. I strive to inspire and encourage them in all aspects of their lives, whether it be through sharing my own experiences, offering advice, or simply being there to listen.

While retirement is often seen as a time to focus on oneself and indulge in personal hobbies and interests, I have found greater fulfillment in dedicating my time and energy to my family. The irony is not lost on me—this stage of life is commonly referred to as "me" time, yet I have chosen to make it about my loved ones. By prioritizing my family, I hope to create a strong foundation of support and love that will carry us through any challenges we may face.

Bobbie's Take:

As Charles embarks on this new chapter of his life—and really it's a new chapter in all of our lives—it's a time to reflect on all that he has given to our family throughout his journey in the military and in his corporate career.

It's clear that he has always been a dedicated and hardworking provider for our family, but retirement offers a new opportunity to give even more in new ways. With the luxury of more flexible time, Charles is able to devote his full attention and energy to what matters most. Now, with Charles present and fully engaged, our family is enjoying a new level of connection, savoring every moment, and looking forward to many more Encore years to come.

Your Encore:

What steps will you take to prioritize your family in your Encore stage?

CHAPTER TWO

FINANCIAL CONCERNS

The Encore stage had finally arrived for Bobbie and me. After decades of hard work, careful planning, and prudent financial management, we were confident that our future was secure. We had faithfully saved, invested wisely, and paid off our debts, including our credit cards. With a solid retirement plan in place, we were ready to embrace a life of leisure, travel, and new experiences.

But life has a way of throwing unexpected curveballs.

I had been considering a new venture in this Encore stage, an opportunity to share my knowledge and expertise in human resources through consulting. It seemed like the perfect way to stay engaged, keep my skills sharp, and contribute to the professional world while enjoying the fruits of retirement. So Bobbie and I took a leap of faith and decided to start our HR consulting business.

It wasn't long before we got the chance to consult with a company on a project that would be right up my alley and also financially rewarding. However, there was a catch.

Unlike the comfortable paychecks and bonus payouts of the past, this engagement would operate on a different timeline. The payment for our services would only come at the end of the project to include net thirty, sixty, or ninety days. Unfortunately, that put us in the position of having to make significant financial commitments without immediate funds set aside to cover them.

We hated to do it, but we leveraged the credit cards that had been carefully paid off before our retirement began. We had planned on using them sparingly, but now they were the only way we could see to start my new venture. We had to book flights, hotel accommodations, and make sure every aspect of the project was funded, organized, and ready to go. The credit card bills with high interest rates began to mount.

As the due date for the unplanned credit card bill approached, a sinking feeling set in. Bobbie and I realized that it would be months before we received the compensation promised for the consulting work. We had walked willingly into this situation, but now the consequences were beginning to reveal themselves. Had stepping outside of our financial plan for retirement jeopardized everything?

Preparing for Retirement

When you retire, you know the regular paychecks are done. You won't receive pay bonuses anymore. Pretty much all of your regularly scheduled income ceases. The money you have saved and ready to tap into is essentially all that's there. You have to live off of it. This is why it is critically important that you have prepared and managed your finances well before your Encore begins.

I grew up poor. Money was hard to come by. My mom and dad taught me and my brother how to value a dollar and how to make money work for us. Having grown up with these values, I learned how to work hard, stay committed to my responsibilities, and manage my money.

I always say that I was blessed to have spent my early career in the military. There was additional pay in the service that helped me pay for my family's bills, and I am grateful for that. I am also grateful to have then joined a company that offered a pension, 401k, and stock. Not many private companies do this today.

In my book, *The Company Doesn't Love You*, I shared how I prepared for my retirement. Early in my career I learned from a certified financial advisor about 401k and began investing money into it. I started putting in as little as 3% of my salary and eventually increased it to 30% over the course of my career. I made a commitment to myself to save and invest. After a few years, I became an executive and received stocks and grants from the company. This allowed me to become financially stable.

My hard work and the decision to save and invest have paid off. The credit card hiccup as we started our new business did not derail us. It was a glitch that we had to deal with, but in general, Bobbie and I are well-positioned for our Encore years.

That doesn't mean we can just sit down, relax, travel the world, and spend our savings. We manage our money and make sure we are happy, stable, and secure.

The reality is, not everyone is well-prepared for the financial challenges of retirement. Your journey through your Career Life Cycle could be very different from mine. While some may have carefully saved, invested wisely, and planned their finances, others find themselves facing unexpected obstacles, uncertain futures, and the harsh realities of financial instability.

I recognize the diversity of experiences around preparing for retirement with empathy, understanding, and a genuine desire to offer guidance and support to those who may find themselves in difficult circumstances.

I want you to know that I'm here to share what I've learned with you, no matter where your own retirement journey has taken you. This isn't about giving you a strict roadmap or a set of rules to follow. Instead, I hope to offer you some helpful insights that can make a difference in your life. Whether you've planned meticulously or found yourself caught off guard by the financial realities of retirement, I believe there's something here for everyone.

Managing Your Finances

Let's face it: managing your finances becomes even more crucial as you enter retirement. Unlike during your working years, there's typically no additional income flowing in. Every dollar you spend is one that you can't replenish. It's important to grasp this reality and use your resources wisely. Gone are the days of big bonuses and salary increases. That's the truth, and it's essential to manage your expectations accordingly. The responsibility falls on your shoulders to do an excellent job of financial management in this new chapter of life.

What I have learned is that if you manage your resources properly and stay disciplined, you can enjoy a fun and worry-free retirement. I'm not saying Bobbie and I are "rich," but we are comfortable because we saved and are careful with our spending.

Bobbie loves to travel and loves the idea that we can travel whenever we want. We can visit extended family members who live long distances away and spend more time with them than we used to. We can also travel to visit our daughters whenever we like. But we don't just buy our tickets and book hotels on a whim. Everything is planned ahead of time. The key is to budget well and follow the plan.

Budget Well

Budgeting remains a crucial aspect of retirement, perhaps even more so than before. It's essential to exercise control over your expenses, resisting the temptation of mindless spending. You can't just splurge on the latest gadgets or throw the credit card down for extravagant purchases without considering the consequences. Living within your means becomes critical because the future is uncertain, and being financially prepared for anything is key.

On the other hand, as you navigate this stage of life, it's equally important to find a balance between financial responsibility and enjoying the benefits that retirement brings. These are the years where you can finally take the time to enjoy the fruits of your labor, pursue your passions, and create meaningful experiences.

Maybe you're already a pro at budgeting. But if you're like the great percentage of people who mistake BUDGET as a four-letter word, here are a few practical tips.

Assess your income and expenses: Start by evaluating your income sources, such as pensions, social security, and any additional investments or part-time work. Then, carefully analyze your expenses, differentiating between essential needs and discretionary wants. This assessment will provide a clear picture of your financial situation and guide your budgeting decisions.

Create a realistic budget: Based on your income and expenses, establish a budget that aligns with your financial goals and priorities. Be realistic and practical, accounting for necessary expenses like housing, healthcare, groceries, and utilities. Set aside some funds for discretionary spending, but make sure it remains within your means.

Be ready for unexpected expenses: Life has a way of throwing surprises at us, and being prepared for unforeseen costs is essential. Create an emergency fund to cover unexpected medical bills, home repairs, or other financial setbacks. Having a safety net will provide peace of mind and protect your overall financial stability.

Minimize debt and manage credit wisely: Retiring with debt can put a strain on your finances. Prioritize paying off high-interest debts, such as credit cards or outstanding loans, as part of your budgeting plan. Avoid accumulating new debt and use credit cards responsibly, paying off the balance in full each month to avoid unnecessary interest charges. (Yes, Bobbie and I learned this one the hard way.)

Continually review and adjust your budget: Financial circumstances may change during retirement, so it's important to regularly review and adjust your budget accordingly. Keep track of your expenses, income, and any fluctuations in your financial situation. Make necessary adjustments to ensure your budget remains effective and aligned with your evolving needs.

While careful budgeting remains crucial, it's vital to embrace the opportunities that retirement offers and find ways to make the most of them. So, find a way to strike that delicate balance, ensuring both financial stability and the chance to savor the richness of these well-deserved years.

Seek Help from a Financial Advisor

If you have investments and saved money for your Encore stage of life, you should have a financial advisor by now. A certified financial advisor will help you plan and ensure that your money gets stretched beyond even a generous life expectancy for you. You might think you already know how to manage your money, but a financial advisor does this for a living and can give you the proper guidance.

As I shared in my book *The Company Doesn't Love You*, Bobbie and I hired a financial advisor way back in 2003. That was when my salary was strong, and I was getting great bonuses and stock in the company. Our advisor taught us how to get the greatest return on our investments and prepare for retirement. We learned about investment and financial planning, and as a result, opened accounts for our daughters and educated them on the importance of financial literacy as well.

If you haven't hired an advisor, ask around in your network for recommendations. Look for someone who is well-grounded, certified, with a history of being successful and honest, and with work experience in a reputable company. In our case, we interviewed three possible advisors before making our decision.

Bobbie and I still meet regularly with our advisor. We cover topics such as retirement goals and lifestyle expectations, income sources and investment strategies, retirement savings and withdrawal strategies, healthcare and long-term care considerations, and finally estate planning and legacy goals.

Remember, these topics are meant to serve as a starting point for discussions with your financial advisor. The specific areas of focus may vary based on your individual circumstances and goals. Openly communicate your concerns, ask questions, and collaborate with your advisor to create a comprehensive retirement plan that aligns with your vision for the future.

Consider Investing

Retirement opens up a window of opportunity for low-risk investments, particularly as you grow older. You want to prioritize preserving your retirement fund rather than chasing aggressive returns during the Encore stage. Just being honest, the older you get, the less time you have to recover from financial losses.

Navigating the world of investing can be complex and unpredictable. Market fluctuations bring both highs and lows, which can be unsettling to someone who constantly watches Wall Street. This is where an investment manager becomes invaluable.

A good investment manager will work with you to create a well-balanced portfolio, making sure that your investments are diversified. By spreading your investments across asset classes, you can manage the impact of a sluggish market and reduce your vulnerability to significant losses.

Remember, as you enter the Encore stage, it's essential to strike a balance between seeking growth and preserving your hard-earned savings. By working with a skilled investment manager, you can navigate the intricacies of the market, ensuring your investment strategy aligns with your financial needs and your goals.

Bobbie's Take:

When Charles retired, we were pretty much debt-free and ready for our Encore. We realized money would not be streaming in, so we had to settle our financial responsibilities. We paid off everything except for the mortgage. We allocated the funds we needed to pay for our daily needs as well as emergencies.

The key to financial health in retirement—and really in all stages of life—is discipline. If I were the type of person to spend everything we earn, we wouldn't be in the position that we're in now where we can enjoy the fruit of our labor.

We learned to live within our means and spend every dollar wisely. Charles and I learned how to navigate our finances, so now we're reaping the benefits.

Having said that, retirement is also a time to have fun and enjoy what you've worked hard for. As you retire, you don't want to be rigid, dreading every moment of retirement, thinking you have to be strictly bound by your budget. Charles and I follow our budget very closely, but we do have fun. We stay disciplined, but we don't have to pinch pennies.

I would add two more things to what Charles has already shared. One, prioritize *experiences* over material possessions. I know it's tempting to splurge on big purchases that you finally have enough money to cover, and lots of people do. But focusing on experiences and creating lasting memories with your partner and even your family will really provide you with greater fulfillment during retirement. I would just encourage you to make sure you budget for travel, pursuing hobbies, spending time with loved ones, or just taking part in activities that bring you joy.

Two, keep an open line of communication with your partner. Every couple knows that finances can be a sensitive topic, so open and regular communication with your partner is crucial. Discuss financial goals, concerns, and decisions together. By finding common ground with regard to money management, you can navigate retirement as a team, which will make things easier all around.

Your Encore

How have you been managing your retirement money? Do you have a budget plan set up? How can you budget your resources to make sure it lasts for a long time? What fun activities have you planned and budgeted for?

Exploring New Opportunities

I recognize that not everyone is in the same position that Bobbie and I are in, having planned for our retirement years before they arrived. Our planning, as well as an opportunity from my company, set me up to retire early at age fifty-three. For me, that's too young to just sit around and enjoy the "golden years," so I had to find something else to do to stay busy, which included creating additional revenue streams.

Many Americans work beyond age sixty-five or sixty-seven (when government retirement benefits kick in, depending on when you were born). For them, sitting around wasn't an option simply because the need for additional income was too great. Either way, there are some interesting options to explore.

Thriving Through Passionate Work

Sometimes, the best solution is to find a fun part-time job that brings in some extra money during retirement. I've seen many retirees who weren't financially secure take on part-time jobs they are passionate about.

At the Encore stage of life, you have the freedom to choose a job you truly enjoy, aligning it with your interests and hobbies. It's no longer about grinding the forty-plus-hour weeks in Corporate America; instead, it becomes a chance to turn your passion into a rewarding part-time income generator.

If you don't know of a part-time job you can explore, maybe you should think about starting your own! Bobbie and I started our consulting business small and slow. We worked pro bono with non-profits to build credibility and a reputation for our company. Our goal was, and still is, to help clients reach their full potential.

Today, we call our venture C&B Consulting LLC, and it is thriving. It is helping us financially, but I don't exactly consider it as just another job. To me, it's a calling, almost a ministry, to give back and inspire others.

Bobbie's and my financial plans for retirement cover our expenses well into our 100s (hey, who knows?!). Do we really *need* the money from our consulting work? Not really, but having that extra income brings us more freedom and allows us to pursue what we enjoy. It's all about continuing to build wealth and doing the things we love, like traveling and visiting family, without having to touch our retirement savings.

Bobbie's Take:

When Charles first told me about his plan to start a business, I was not happy at all, to be honest. He said it would be an HR-related venture, but that was his career field, and I didn't know anything about HR, being in the financial field most of my life. It wasn't my passion, and I didn't see a need.

In the beginning, it was difficult, and we had some very hard times. I was not happy until I finally changed my mindset and decided to try a different approach to make it work. That's when I started the recruitment component of our company, and that became my part of our HR business.

I talk to younger people and help them get started in their careers. I love doing that. It's my way of giving back, and it is very rewarding. I guess that's the key—you have to embrace a positive mindset and make your own happiness.

When Charles retired, I thought we were not going to work anymore. We'd just live on the retirement savings, do things around the house, and travel a little bit. But, no. We decided to start a company as a way to help people and continue the revenue stream. And what a great decision that has proved to be!

Your Encore

What are your hobbies and passions? What type of Encore work would you be interested in?

CHAPTER THREE

FEARS

In the Encore stage of life, common fears can arise, casting a shadow of uncertainty over our transition into retirement. Let's explore some of the more common fears and some ways to mitigate them.

Fear of the Unknown

My greatest fear in approaching the Encore stage was the fear of the unknown, and as far as I could see, there was no way around that fear. I started working when I was twelve years old, a dutiful young Mississippi boy who was full of dreams. For more than three decades, I worked hard, and then, all of a sudden, the daily grind in the office stopped. What would my future hold?

As you read in Chapter Two, I had planned for my retirement well. I was ready financially. I saved enough and invested wisely so that my wife and I would not worry about money. And yet, there I was, uncertain and a little fearful about what might actually happen next that I couldn't predict.

For years I have had the satisfaction of providing well for my wife and daughters. Being the provider, the primary source of income for my family, I took pride in my work. From my time in the military through my entire tenure at Kraft, I was able to envision and even plan for my career moves. I could visualize my career goals and map potential strategies for achieving them. But I didn't have a clear picture of this retirement thing. I couldn't see around the corner.

This sudden inability to have a solid grasp on what life would hold in the next few years left me feeling unstable, on shaky ground, and not sure how to manage those feelings. After being so sure-footed and certain throughout my entire career, this threw me for a loop and took me on a slippery slope into a darker place of insecurity and anxiety.

Bobbie's Take:

As Charles mentioned earlier, I was concerned he might be slipping into depression after retirement. He pulled back from our usual family interactions and became very quiet. It was almost like he wasn't there. He wasn't engaged. Charles changed, and I could see it. He was struggling every day, but he couldn't put a name to what was going on.

I wasn't sure of what was really going on with him at that point. I never worried about his confidence and state of mind before he retired. He was great as an executive, and I always felt secure with him and his work. But when it came to being retired, it was a whole new world for him—and for me. Given his seeming uncertainty and possible depression, I started to have my own doubts, and that's where the fear came in for me.

Your Encore

As you enter the Encore stage, do you see yourself pulling back from your usual daily life rhythms? What personality changes are you going through? Are you afraid to tell people about what you are going through at the moment?

Fear of Outliving Your Money

The fear of outliving your savings is common among retirees. As I've always said, I was blessed with a unique and fulfilling career history. My experiences in the military and working as an executive for Kraft opened up opportunities for me to earn, put a good sum of money into my 401k, and invest in stocks.

Although I felt confident our resources would see Bobbie and me through retirement, I was still somewhat anxious. Living without a guaranteed monthly income is a drastic change, no matter how much that income was to begin with. What if something unexpected happened to drain our resources, such as needing long-term assisted living or intense medical care? Would we outlive our savings?

A study conducted by The Hartford Financial Services Group Inc. and the Massachusetts Institute of Technology AgeLab[1] revealed that Americans (87% of respondents) fear retirement because they lack that guaranteed income and aren't sure what they have set aside for this stage of life will carry them through.

The reality is, many Americans are truly not financially prepared for retirement—20% of respondents said they have nothing at all saved while less than half (47%) have access to a pension plan that could help supplement Social Security. In these cases, the fear of outliving resources is amplified and, unfortunately, likely.

Bobbie's Take:

When Charles retired, I got a little nervous. Charles has always been a good provider. A certain amount of income was always coming in, and when it stopped, I wondered if we would have enough for the years we have left.

I initially wondered if I should go back to work. I really didn't want us to go back to the time early in our marriage when we struggled financially. I didn't want to experience the hardship again after we had made it so far and succeeded in our careers. I didn't want to go backward.

Fortunately, we have a good financial advisor who was able to talk me off the cliff, so to speak, and show me that we were not likely to run out of our savings, and would even have a strong inheritance to leave our daughters someday.

Your Encore

Are you like most Americans, worried that you might outlive your savings? How confident are you in your current financial preparedness for retirement, considering the lack of guaranteed income and potential gaps in savings or pension plans?

Fear of Starting Over with Your Spouse

To be honest, one of my greatest concerns approaching retirement was the prospect of staying at home with my wife all the time. Bobbie and I have been married for thirty-six years but only had two years alone together before our daughters arrived. We needed to get back together and restart our marriage, and that scared me. I was sure I would have a hard time figuring this thing out.

Half of our friends are retired and divorced. They are our age and, like us, have been married for a long time. When they got to the point of retirement, a lot of them got divorced, and so in my mind, the fear of retiring was creeping in because of that. I love Bobbie, but as with most married couples, we have our adverse moments!

For more than thirty years, our life together wasn't about us. It was about our two daughters. They were the center of our universe. After retirement, life was not about the kids anymore. Reintroducing ourselves to each other was not easy, so we decided to talk things through with a therapist. Communication is very important.

Bobbie's Take

We saw a therapist, and there is no shame in that. We wanted to make things work between us, so we sought help and found it. Now we are in a better place and loving our life. We have common goals—to succeed in our business, to serve our clients, to stay healthy for as long as we can, to help people, to write books, to travel, to visit family, and to do all these together.

But we are also exploring new ways to have fun together. For example, we've started visiting restaurants that we've never been to before. We go on long walks with no particular destination in mind, just to enjoy nature and each other's company. We've taken vacations without our daughters for the first time, and that's been a whole new experience for us, too. In general, we've adopted a new sense of adventure, and are excited to see where that will lead us in the years to come.

Your Encore

How are you getting along with your spouse now that you have an empty nest? Do you like each other's company as much as you love one another? Would you benefit from working through some bumps in the road with a licensed therapist or counselor?

Fear of Poor Health and Untimely Death

This fear is a big one. A lot of the males in my family passed away early. They suffered from colon cancer, prostate cancer, heart disease, and other terminal illnesses. This has always haunted me, especially when I turned forty.

When I was younger, health wasn't on my list of top priorities. But when I was nearing my Encore stage, the inevitable became more real and alarming. I was afraid I wouldn't see retirement, and this was one of the reasons why I retired early. I felt like everyone else in my family barely made it to retirement age, and those that did make it passed away early.

I am a man of faith. I believe in God, Heaven, and the afterlife. Like many people I know, I see death as not the end, but of the beginning of our eternal life.

The same study I mentioned earlier conducted by The Hartford Financial Services Group and the Massachusetts Institute of Technology AgeLab revealed that a great number of Americans are actually *more* afraid of retirement than dying.

I think what I am really more afraid of are the pains and agony associated with being sick and dying. And again, the fear of the unknown comes into play, not knowing what could happen to my loved ones after I pass away. The thought of breaking your family's heart when you pass can keep you up all night.

Bobbie's Take:

I completely agree with Charles on this. He's spot on. Poor health and untimely death are a big fear of people our age. Our family members did die early, and I've always known in the back of my mind that this was a major fear for Charles.

We can't do anything about that, but what I did do was encourage him to work out and stay healthy. That was my big contribution as his wife in addressing this fear. And we still work out today. When you are retired, that is one thing you must do because it helps with your overall health, psyche, and outlook in life.

Your Encore

Do you have a family history of family members dying early? Have you taken any steps to address or mitigate the fear of dying early in retirement, such as purchasing life insurance or considering alternative financial strategies to protect your family?

Preparing to Minimize the Impact of Fear when Retiring

✓ Get Health Checks

When I turned forty, I became more mindful of my health. I started having colonoscopies at forty-five, the age recommended by my doctor. Like my relatives before me, I was afraid I could suffer from colorectal cancer. My first colonoscopy turned out clear, but I took it again after three years and will continue to do so.

✓ Work Out

Bobbie kept bugging me to get proper exercise and work out. "You need to at least walk," she often said. When I was still grinding away in Corporate America, I didn't have the time to regularly exercise. But now I do. My wife got me a gym membership, and I've been exercising regularly since. Any form of physical activity helps improve mental health, emotional, psychological, and social well-being, as well as cognitive functions. Bobbie was right. We can take care of our overall well-being by working out when we can—even if it's just walking.

✓ Plan to move forward

As you are about to retire, make sure to come up with a plan before making your Encore. In the preceding chapter, I suggested ways to prepare financially for retirement: manage your money, budget well, seek help from a financial advisor, and consider investing. Doing this will give you a buffer of confidence for you and your family. The fear of outliving your money might still be there, but you will have greater peace of mind.

Embrace your retirement instead of running from it. Retirement is inevitable, and getting there becomes more difficult if you don't embrace it right away. I was in denial for some time, and it could have ruined my marriage.

✓ Plan with your spouse

If couples talked and planned ahead of retirement, they could spare themselves from a lot of heartaches, a lot of suffering, and a lot of misunderstandings. They could identify their fears early on and see how they might be able to navigate around or through them.

If you have a plan and agree on a way to tackle retirement together, you're going to be closer to each other. You're bringing your relationship back to where you were before the kids. You had a dream back when you were young, and now you can rekindle that dream and work together to achieve it.

✓ Shift Your Mindset: Embrace a Stress-free Life

I have lived a fairly stressful life. Most of my adult life was about working, performing, earning, meeting deadlines, and doing this and that. Just thinking about it now is causing me stress. When I retired, I held on to that lifestyle for a time. My mind was so conditioned for getting things done right that I stressed about the smallest of things.

I knew I had to change, but it took me about five years for the shift in mindset to really happen because the corporate lifestyle was so ingrained. Initially, I felt like I had to get up at 5:00 or 5:30 every morning. I felt I needed to move around and get some things done.

Just recently, I finally made myself enjoy sleep and get up at 8:30. I was amazed and thought, "Wow, I didn't know waking up this late was even possible." That felt good. *I felt good.*

Today, I'm learning to slow things down and not move as fast mentally, and it's okay.

✓ Take up a Hobby

In the Encore stage, discovering fulfilling hobbies is more than just a pastime; it's a vital ingredient for a happy and purposeful life. Engaging in activities like volunteering or pursuing passions like music not only provides a sense of fulfillment but also promotes mental and emotional well-being. Hobbies offer opportunities for social interaction, skill development, and personal growth, helping retirees stay active, connected, and mentally agile. Whether it's strumming a guitar, lending a hand to a charitable cause, or exploring new interests, retirement becomes a time to embrace newfound passions and discover the endless joys that come with them.

Fears of Different Demographic Points of View

I believe culture, race, and other factors affect the way you look at retirement. Here is a quick look at some data that will explain how Americans view retirement and what makes them fearful.

- **African Americans:** Many African Americans fear retirement due to long-standing income and wealth disparities along with low percentages of people who save. Generally, Black families tend to have lower average incomes than White families. According to the Society for Financial Education and Professional Development, Inc.[2], African Americans don't normally participate in retirement accounts or the stock market. Many simply rely on Social Security.

- **Latin Americans:** A recent study by the National Institute on Retirement Security[3] said Latinos are the least prepared financially for retirement. Four out of five Hispanic households have less than $10,000 in retirement savings. Also, Latino workers are normally in low-wage jobs in the private sector and are less likely to have access to retirement plans.
- **Asian Americans:** Asian Americans are very focused on their financial goals leading to retirement, based on the Asian American Retirement Risk Study[4]. They are also unlikely to commit bad financial behaviors that reduce retirement savings, such as making withdrawals and taking hardship loans.
- **Gender, Age, Married/Unmarried:** Again, citing The Hartford Financial Services Group and the Massachusetts Institute of Technology AgeLab research[5], women are more fearful of retirement than men. Eighty-three percent of women surveyed are worried about inflation, 75% are concerned about poor health in retirement, and 64% are worried about outliving their money. Meanwhile, younger people fear retirement more than those who are close to retiring.

Finally, I find it interesting to know that adults who were married once are less likely to have zero retirement savings and more likely to have $100,000 or more in savings. They are better off than those who have never been married and those who have been married two or more times[6].

Fear of the unknown looms large as we approach the Encore stage of our lives. Retirement brings with it a multitude of uncertainties and concerns that can cause anxiety and stress. Whether it's the fear of outliving our savings, the fear of poor health and untimely death, or the fear of starting over with our spouse, these fears are real and valid.

However, it is essential to confront and address these fears in order to navigate retirement successfully. By planning ahead, seeking financial advice, and engaging in open communication with our partners, we can minimize the impact of these fears.

Embracing a stress-free mindset and shifting our perspective to see retirement as an opportunity for personal growth and fulfillment can make the transition smoother. It is also important to recognize that different demographic groups may face unique challenges and fears in retirement, which should be taken into consideration.

By understanding these fears and learning from the experiences of others, we can better prepare ourselves for the uncertainties that lie ahead. Ultimately, the Encore stage is a new chapter in our lives, and with proper planning and a positive mindset, we can make it a fulfilling and joyful phase of our journey.

CHAPTER FOUR

FAITH

In this short chapter, I'll be sharing about my faith and how it is giving me purpose and happiness in retirement. I understand some people may not be comfortable reading or hearing about someone else's personal faith system or religion, so if you prefer to skip past this chapter, that's always an option.

My reason for faith is not based on any religion or church. Although my father is a pastor, and I grew up going to Sunday school, it was my personal experiences that solidified my personal belief in God.

In my book, *The Company Doesn't Love You*, I shared in great detail how I could have been killed in a car accident if not for a soft voice in my head that said, "Don't buckle your seatbelt."

The short version is this: As I was crossing through a green light at an intersection, a semi-truck pulling a trailer ran the red light heading straight for the side of my SUV. The same soft voice said, "Lay down across the passenger seat. You're going to be OK. Lay down." I immediately threw myself all the way down and blacked out.

When I came to, I was pinned down in my sideways position in the wreckage. The roof of my car was crushed. Miraculously, I survived this horrific accident that could have left me decapitated. What's incredible was that I had nothing broken, no cuts—not even a scratch!

I was rushed to the hospital, and it was there where a police officer told me, "An angel was with you today." She explained that if I had been buckled in, I would have died. The seatbelt would not have allowed me to lie down across the passenger seat.

I believe it was Divine intervention that preserved me that day. I believe it was my faith and relationship with God that saved my life. On that particular day, it wasn't my time. There was more for me to do and still have an Encore to perform in life.

Faith and Purpose in Retirement

Looking back, it is clear to me that the way I view family is founded on my mother's amazing faith. My dad is a pastor, but my mom is certainly the matriarch of the community. She really is the rock. Even today, as it was when we were little, my mom is the type of person who calls each one of us every week just to say a prayer with us. Every week! And she doesn't just do this for her kids and grandkids, but also for all the people in the community.

She's been doing that for as long as I can remember. And ever since she figured out how to use the smartphone and how to text, she's been sending text messages to probably thirty different people every morning with a word of encouragement or a Bible verse for the day.

I love that. I pray she continues to be such an example of what it means to live out your faith because it lights that fire under Bobbie and me to make sure we are living out our God-given purpose in life.

Today, I'm really focused on leaving a similar legacy of faith. I want to be an example, a positive role model. This now is my purpose in life. I try to be a living, walking testimony so that people will see my faith in everything I do.

My focus is still primarily on family, but when I talk to my friends, to my fraternity brothers, and when I speak at events, I tell them I want to give honor to God and to thank Him for having allowed me to experience a great life. I would not be where I am today without Him.

I don't walk around with a Bible trying to tell everybody what to do and what to believe in. But I do tell people I'm humbled, grateful, and blessed for my faith in God. I even do it sometimes in my emails and on social media.

I don't shove religion on anybody, but I do encourage you to have faith. You can believe whatever it is you want to believe in as long as it will help you to become a better person and move you forward toward your purpose in life.

Faith, the Antidote to the Fears Most Americans Face in Retirement

✓ Faith to Face the Unknown

Scriptures define faith this way: It is confidence in what we hope for and assurance about what we do not see (Ephesians 11:1-2). In other words, faith somehow makes you see what you cannot see, know what you do not know. It is my faith that gives me peace and strength to face my greatest fear in retirement—the unknown.

The more fearful I became, the stronger my faith grew. I'm walking more in faith every day now than I did before. When I get up in the morning, I really take time to meditate to get closer to God and be comfortable with myself. There's no stress when I do that. I used to listen to jazz and R & B music, but now I find myself listening to gospel music more and more.

I realized that since it was faith that brought me to where I am now, it is also faith that will take me through the unknown. Faith has been a part of my daily life, my life journey, so why give up now? Why exclude it now when I need it more than ever?

Bobbie's Take:

I completely agree with Charles that you need something in your life that you have faith in. I'm not saying you have to believe in my God or follow our spiritual preference. When my daughters were in high school, they were free to explore their faith through different denominations, but we always kept the door open to join us in our worship. Whatever makes you reflect on life and get spiritual relief, go for it.

Your Encore

How is your faith life? Does it make you less fearful about the unknown? What might you do to establish a kind of faith that will give you the courage to face your fears?

✓ Faith that Keeps Us Together

Bobbie and I are practicing Christians. We are leaders in our church, and it's been like that for years. Faith in God has always been part of our marriage, and I believe it's one of the things that kept us together. We love our lives at church together. We've always been involved with small groups. We now actually lead a ministry at church involving professionals. We provide advice and help kids prepare for college. We also coach people on how to write resumes and how to ace an interview. We try to show others how they can be successful in areas where they wish to be. That's how we give back to our church. And being partners in ministry makes us appreciate each other more.

Bobbie's Take:

I love leading the ministry with Charles, especially helping young people just getting started in their careers and also helping professionals reinvent their careers.

When we decided to retire, I needed my faith to help me get through it all. It was my faith that I leaned on in the most difficult moments in retirement. I will say that if you do not have some type of faith, you will not experience any form of spiritual relief, which is so important for you to have access to.

Your Encore

In what specific ways do you serve within your faith community? How has your involvement in serving impacted your personal spiritual growth and deepened your connection to your faith?

✓ Faith in People to Take Care of My Money

In a slightly different take on the concept of faith, it also takes a lot of faith to hand over your hard-earned money to a company or a person to manage for you. Because of our long-standing relationship, I have complete faith in our financial advisor and his capability to handle my money. But I also trust that God led us to this person and will allow us to live in financial security.

Bobbie and I tithe our income to the church, and we've never missed a beat. That's what the Bible says, and I have complete faith in my church that my tithes and offerings go to the homeless or whoever is in need of help. I believe that if you do these things, what you gave will come back way more than you can dream of. And that's been our faith and beliefs.

Bobbie's Take:

In some cases, African-Americans are hesitant to trust other people with their money. They oftentimes just don't feel comfortable putting their money in a bank or giving it to a financial institution to manage.

When Charles first suggested we hand over our money to a financial advisor, it wasn't that I didn't trust the advisor. At the time, I felt we needed to have that money readily available in case of an unexpected financial need.

In the end, it has turned out great, so I'd say having faith enough to trust when God leads you to steward your finances a certain way is important. And have faith in whom He leads you to for help! (But still, do your homework in researching that person or company!)

Your Encore

How does your faith influence your decision-making when it comes to financial matters, such as budgeting, saving, and charitable giving? In what ways do you prioritize aligning your financial choices with your faith values and principles?

✓ Faith in the Storms

I believe that in life you are always in one of three places: you are either about to enter a storm, you are in a storm, or you are coming out of the storm. In all three situations, you can draw strength and find peace when you exercise your faith.

When facing problems, illnesses, deadlines, financial instability, death in the family, snags in relationships, or anything else, you must understand these are life storms and faith will see you through them. When you are coming out of the storm, you can look back and see how faith carried you, and then thank God and the people who helped you.

That's been my thought process. Life on this green earth will end, and when I get to the other side, I will say, "Hey, faith brought me through."

 **Bobbie's Take:**

When you are working, you don't really have as much time to go to church and grow spiritually. Like Charles said, now that we have time, our faith has amplified. And the more we amplify our belief, we become more calm, more grateful, and more at ease. We don't have to worry about being retired and what's going to happen next. We are at a good place in our life. My faith has really made me grow, more so now than ever.

Your Encore

During challenging or turbulent times in your life, how does your faith serve as a source of strength and guidance? What specific beliefs or practices help you navigate through the storms?

Faith has been an integral part of my life, giving me purpose and happiness in retirement. While I understand that discussing personal faith may not resonate with everyone, I wanted to share how it has shaped my journey.

Today, my focus is on being a living testimony and honoring God in all that I do. Faith has become the antidote to my fears and has provided me with the strength and perspective to face the unknown. It has strengthened my marriage and guided my financial decisions.

Whether it is in times of peace or storms, faith remains a constant source of strength and guidance, allowing me to navigate through life with peace and gratitude. I encourage you to explore your own faith journey and discover the ways it can bring purpose, peace, and fulfillment to your retirement and beyond.

CHAPTER FIVE

FRICTION

As I stepped onto the lush green fairway of the golf course, a sense of tranquility washed over me. The morning sun painted a golden hue on the manicured landscape. It was a scene that invited relaxation and enjoyment. And yet, the atmosphere held a subtle tension, a silent reminder that I was an anomaly in this realm of privilege and tradition.

I made my way to the first tee with a few pairs of curious eyes following me. I knew the thoughts that swirled in their minds. Having spent the majority of my corporate career as one of only a few people of color in upper-level management positions, I had grown accustomed to these glances, the unspoken judgments that attempted to confine me to a preconceived notion of who I should be and where I should belong. Equally important, I learned how to be comfortable in uncomfortable situations.

The glances I received were not overtly hostile or confrontational, but they carried an unmistakable weight. It was as if the unspoken question hung in the air, "What are you doing out here right now?" It was a reminder that biases and stereotypes, though they may evolve and take on different forms, continue to permeate our lives even in retirement.

It wasn't just my race that set me apart; it was also my age. Being relatively young-ish looking in a sea of, shall we say, more "senior" golfers raised eyebrows and fueled curiosity. As I played through the course, I couldn't help but think about the broader implications of these biases. If they show up here on the golf course, where else do they show up in the Encore stage? What other barriers and limitations do they put on our ability to fully embrace this stage of life?

It is a stark reminder that biases and stereotypes don't simply quit when we leave the working world; they continue to shape our experiences, just in different ways.

Encore-Related Challenges

The fifth and final element of the Life Fulfillment Framework as it pertains to the Encore stage is Friction. In my book, *The Company Doesn't Love You*, I describe Friction as the stereotypes and biases individuals often encounter in the workplace based on factors such as their race, gender, or any other distinguishing characteristic.

As much as I wish it weren't the case, Friction doesn't magically disappear once retirement is reached; it continues outside of the workplace, even beyond the traditional working years. In the Encore stage, Friction can manifest in new (and not-so-new) challenges.

Friction in this stage most often manifests in ageism, classicism, sexism, and/or racism. Retirees from marginalized backgrounds may find it difficult to access resources and opportunities that can enhance their retirement experience. Let's take a look at each of these four areas a little more closely.

Ageism

✓ Prejudice or discrimination against people based on their age.

My corporate job was coming to an end based on an early retirement agreement I reached with the organization I had been with for more than twenty-five years. It was a great option for me financially—a no brainer, really.

However, I was only fifty-three years old, so some doubts started to creep in about whether I should really cease working in Corporate America altogether, or if I should look for a new job to get me through a few more years until I was closer to what is generally considered to be retirement age.

Given my position as a VP of Human Resources in a Fortune 500 company, and with my proven track record of success, I figured someone would snatch me up pretty quickly. I went ahead and sent out dozens of resumes and letters of interest, figuring I'd have plenty of options coming back my way.

I got two call-backs.

Having dealt with the unconscious bias around race for the entirety of my career, my first assumption was that somehow I was being overlooked for that reason. Yet nothing about my resume would have indicated my race, so I was a little perplexed. You'd think if that was a factor it would've shown up after they met me face-to-face.

That's when it hit me. Between listing my graduation date on my resume and the dates on my work history, anyone looking at my qualifications would quickly observe that I was within just a few years of retirement.

And if I'm honest, as a Human Resources person, there's a good chance I would have taken note of that same fact on a resume as well, and probably unconsciously given that candidate a lower spot on the totem pole than someone more mid-career level.

Ageism is a pervasive issue in the job market. According to a study by AARP, nearly two-thirds of workers between the ages of forty-five and seventy-four have experienced age discrimination in their workplace or job search[1]. In fact, the Equal Employment Opportunity Commission (EEOC) received over 20,000 age-related discrimination charges in a recent year[2]. These numbers highlight the significant impact of age bias on employment opportunities.

Furthermore, a study conducted by the National Bureau of Economic Research found that older workers are oftentimes perceived as having lower productivity and are less likely to be considered for job openings compared to younger candidates, even when their qualifications are similar[3]. These biases can have a detrimental effect on older job seekers, limiting their chances of securing meaningful employment and contributing their skills and expertise to the workforce.

These statistics and findings shed light on the real consequences of ageism in the job market. The bias and lower priority that I experienced firsthand serve as a stark reminder of the ongoing challenges faced by older workers, even those with impressive credentials and a wealth of experience.

Bobbie's Take:

Ageism permeates every aspect of our society, and its impact on older individuals is undeniable, even when it occurs unconsciously. The corporate world, in particular, seems to be deeply ingrained with biases against older people. As someone who helps people of all ages with their job search, I have witnessed firsthand the power of combating ageism through some simple yet impactful strategies. One key piece of advice I always impart to the people I support is to carefully consider the structure of their resumes. I emphasize that they no longer need to include the year of their graduation, or the dates associated with their early career, as that will introduce unconscious bias to the process.

Your Encore:

Have you ever encountered or witnessed ageism? How can you promote inclusivity and fairness for individuals of all ages in society as a whole?

Classicism or Class Discrimination

✓ Prejudice or discrimination on the basis of social class.

Those who spend the majority of their career in hourly-wage jobs or lower-salary positions often find themselves grappling with significant Friction as they approach retirement. The challenges faced by retirees from these backgrounds are compounded by the fact that they are frequently offered inferior retirement packages and fewer, if any, benefits.

For many individuals in hourly-wage or lower-salary jobs, retirement planning may not have been a viable option due to financial constraints. Limited income and minimal savings make it difficult to build a substantial nest egg for retirement. As a result, retirees from these backgrounds often find themselves in precarious financial situations, struggling to make ends meet during their later years.

Furthermore, the lack of comprehensive retirement benefits, such as employer-sponsored pensions or robust healthcare coverage, further spotlights the classicism faced by retirees from lower-wage jobs. The absence of these crucial resources places additional strain on their financial security and overall well-being.

If you have reached retirement age and face financial challenges or outright class discrimination due to a history of low-income jobs, there are steps you can take to improve your financial security and well-being during the Encore stage.

First, take an in-depth look at your current expenses and identify areas where you can reduce costs and stretch your retirement income without sacrificing essential needs. Make sure to explore all available retirement benefits, including Social Security, pension plans, and other government assistance programs. If you take the time to understand the eligibility rules, you are in a better position to take advantage of the benefits you are entitled to receive.

Connect with local community organizations that offer support to retirees from low-income backgrounds. They may provide resources and services such as affordable housing options, food assistance, healthcare programs, and financial education workshops.

Many retirees explore part-time work options or freelance opportunities to supplement their retirement income. My brother-in-law spent his thirty-five year career with the same company working in shipping. He earned a pension, but decided to take a post-retirement part-time job at the local hardware store to both supplement that pension income and to stay busy and engaged six days a week. If you go this route, look for roles that align with your skills, interests, and availability, allowing you to earn additional income while enjoying a flexible schedule.

And finally, no matter your "class" or income level, it's a great idea to connect with others in a similar position in your community. Look for local senior centers, community groups, and organizations that offer services tailored to retirees. They may provide support networks and resources to help overcome class discrimination and navigate the challenges of retirement on a limited income.

Bobbie's Take:

No matter where your income falls, you can prepare for retirement. With all of the free resources available out there to assist lower-income individuals or families, there really is no reason to be caught empty-handed when the time comes.

The Social Security Administration provides valuable information and resources regarding Social Security benefits, retirement planning, and eligibility. Their website (ssa.gov) offers tools, calculators, and publications to help people understand their benefits and make informed decisions.

Check with local government agencies, community centers, or nonprofit organizations for free financial literacy programs specifically tailored to low-income individuals. These programs provide education on budgeting, saving, investing, and retirement planning.

In this day and age, you can Google search for free retirement planning tools, such as retirement calculators and budgeting apps. Examples include AARP's Retirement Calculator and the U.S. Department of Labor's Retirement Savings Toolkit.

And don't forget your public library! They offer a wealth of free resources, including books, ebooks, and audiobooks on personal finance, retirement planning, and investment strategies. They may also host workshops or seminars on financial topics that can benefit individuals with limited income.

Your Encore:

How has your income level and career path influenced your retirement planning, and what specific challenges do you anticipate or currently face as a result? What steps can you take to maximize the available resources and support for retirees with lower incomes, such as community organizations, financial literacy programs, and online tools?

Sexism

✓ Prejudice or discrimination on the basis of gender.

Sexism in the Encore stage falls heavily against women. Traditional gender roles often dictate that women take on caregiving responsibilities, resulting in interrupted career paths, lower wages, and limited access to employer-sponsored retirement benefits.

As a consequence, women tend to have smaller retirement savings and pensions compared to their male counterparts. The gender pay gap persists throughout a woman's working life, further exacerbating financial disparities in retirement.

Sexism can also manifest in societal expectations and ageist attitudes, devaluing the experiences, wisdom, and contributions of older women.

I think it's appropriate to invite Bobbie to speak up first on this topic!

Bobbie's Take:

When I started my career in corporate America, I aimed to earn as much money as possible to secure our future. But soon I realized that there was a difference in how men and women were treated in terms of pay. Women, especially women of color, faced even greater challenges.

In the early days of our marriage, I made more money than Charles. However, we decided to switch roles. Charles took the lead in his career, climbing the corporate ladder, while I supported him as we moved around the country for each and every promotion he received. I understood my role was to take care of our children and be there for the family.

There were times I questioned my contributions to my family, feeling inadequate compared to Charles since I wasn't contributing equally to our finances. I had taken care of our family, but I still felt like I needed to do more to be equal. It was hard juggling work and family responsibilities while dealing with these feelings.

It was challenging finding a balance between work and family, but I realized that true equality is about more than money.

In addition to the challenges of pay disparity and balancing work and family responsibilities, I know there are other ways sexism can play a role in creating bias during the Encore stage. Society tends to prioritize youth, leading to assumptions that older women are less capable, less relevant, or less deserving of opportunities solely based on our age and gender.

I have realized the importance of being aware of these biases and advocating for myself. It is crucial for me to assert my voice, ensuring that my experiences as a woman are acknowledged and valued throughout our Encore stage.

Charles's Response

And now here is my take on that. As the provider, I wasn't looking for equal contribution. When we agreed she would be focused primarily on raising the girls, that was very important. I saw the value in what she was bringing by taking care of our daughters and me. I really love, appreciate and respect Bobbie for that.

It's important for all of us to educate ourselves about the realities of sexism and its manifestations in the Encore stage. By staying informed, we can be more attuned to the biases that exist and take proactive steps to combat them. This may involve questioning our own assumptions and beliefs, challenging societal norms, and advocating for gender equality in our interactions with others.

Your Encore:

How have the gender pay gap and traditional gender roles impacted your own career or your partner's career and retirement planning? Have you experienced any challenges or disparities as a result? How can you personally contribute to combating sexism and promoting gender equality during the Encore stage?

Racism

✓ Prejudice or discrimination on the basis of ethnicity.

Racism has far-reaching implications that extend beyond the realms of employment and daily life, impacting various aspects of retirement as well. It is important to shed light on the ways in which racism manifests during the Encore stage.

There is a common assumption that all Black Americans solely rely on social security for their income in retirement. However, the reality is far more complex. Within my own community, including my relatives back where I grew up in Mississippi, many are trapped in the cycle of living paycheck to paycheck. As we transitioned into this Encore phase of life, they questioned how Bobbie and I were able to achieve what we have without continuing to work.

Let me be clear: it can be done. The unfortunate truth is that many people of color are not aware of the possibilities. The lack of accessible financial education within our upbringing compounds the challenge. Our parents, like many others, did not possess the tools to guide us in these matters.

As an African-American, I understand the unique challenges we face. Enduring and embracing discomfort has become an inherent part of our journey. We have worked tirelessly, not relying on mere luck, but rather sacrificing much in life. We have been blessed, but our achievements are a result of deliberate decisions made earlier in life, driven by discipline and long-term vision. We played the long game, refusing to give in to instant gratification.

Racial bias also continues to influence the availability and quality of retirement benefits. African-Americans and other minority groups often face barriers in accessing pension plans and other retirement benefits. They may encounter disparities in contribution rates and investment options. These inequities not only affect the financial security of retirees but also their overall well-being during the Encore stage.

Another aspect where racism can manifest in retirement is through social connections and community support. Racial segregation and social exclusion can result in limited networks and resources. Minority individuals may face challenges in finding inclusive and supportive communities, senior centers, or organizations that cater to their unique needs. The absence of such networks can lead to feelings of isolation and hinder opportunities for meaningful engagement and social fulfillment during retirement.

And finally, healthcare disparities rooted in racism can impact retirees' physical and mental well-being. Access to quality healthcare, including preventive care, chronic disease management, and mental health services, may be compromised for minority groups. These disparities can contribute to poorer health outcomes and increased healthcare costs, ultimately affecting the quality of life during retirement.

Bobbie's Take:

One aspect that Charles mentioned, and I wholeheartedly agree with, is the importance of stepping out of our comfort zones and embracing connections with people from diverse backgrounds. This practice has been truly transformative for us. We have cultivated the ability to navigate various environments with ease and find comfort in unfamiliar situations. And let me clarify, this principle is not exclusive to any specific racial or ethnic group. It applies to everyone, regardless of their background.

Life presents uncomfortable situations to each and every one of us, regardless of our race, ethnicity, or any other identifier. Embracing discomfort and learning to navigate through these moments is where genuine growth occurs. It is an essential part of our collective journey as human beings. By challenging ourselves to step outside of our comfort zones and interact with diverse groups, we create opportunities for personal and societal development.

In our own experiences, we have learned that genuine connections and personal growth flourish when we embrace discomfort. We have discovered that we can enter any environment with confidence, whether it's social, professional, or cultural. This ability has enriched our lives and broadened our perspectives, enabling us to build bridges of understanding and empathy with people from all walks of life.

Overcoming Biases

Throughout my career in Corporate America, I refused to let the color of my skin define my worth, and this mindset remains unchanged as I embrace retirement. In my book, *The Company Doesn't Love You*, I shared my battles with what I called the "Prove It Again Bias." I felt that some individuals attributed my success solely to chance due to my skin color.

Today, even though I no longer feel the need to prove myself to anyone, I am aware of the disbelief surrounding our accomplishments as Bobbie and I thrive in retirement. People, including both White individuals and even fellow African-Americans, observe us and wonder, "How can they achieve that? Are they genuinely retired? How have they found success?"

Another bias that I discussed in my book is the "All Eyes Are on Me Bias." Even now, I often sense that I am constantly under scrutiny, as if every move I make is being closely watched. However, I have come to understand that Bobbie and I belong to a small group in terms of our skin color combined with our financial success. People believe that we can't understand or relate to the struggles they face, oblivious to the fact that we endured similar hardships during our pre-retirement years. The distinction is in our refusal to allow those struggles to define or control us.

Our journey serves as a testament to the resilience and determination that allowed us to triumph over adversities. We understand the struggles that individuals face, and our empathy is rooted in shared experiences. We chose not to be defined by our circumstances but to forge our own path, committed to supporting one another. Our story demonstrates the power of perseverance and unity in the face of challenges, inspiring others to persevere and overcome obstacles on their own unique journeys.

AFTERWORD

MY ENCORE

As I wrapped up writing this book, I had a moment of reflection and realized something pretty important: It was during the Encore stage of my life that I became the author of five books, including the one you're holding right now.

I never saw myself as a writer before the Encore stage. I never had the time or chance to write a book when I was caught up in the corporate world. But deep down, I always had this desire to write.

Fifteen years ago, I shared with Bobbie my dream of writing a book that could help others going through life, career, and retirement, so they wouldn't struggle as much as we did. I wanted to leave behind the wisdom I gained about family, faith, finances, fears, and all the challenges that come our way.

I also became an entrepreneur during the Encore stage. Bobbie and I set up our consulting firm before retiring, but it was only after we left our regular jobs that it really took off.

Let me tell you, it wasn't easy. It took hard work, discipline, and a whole lot of faith to make it all happen. But here we are, leaving a legacy behind to help others navigate their career and post-career journeys.

I've always asked myself some deep questions along the way: What's my purpose in life? Who have I helped? What positive change have I made? What difference did I leave behind?

If you take a moment to look at your own life, you'll see the day you were born and imagine the day you'll leave this world. And in between, there's that question: *What did I do? What's my legacy for others?*

I hope my sharing of the lessons I've learned along the way inspires you. It's not going to be a cakewalk; it's going to be a challenge, just like life itself. But if Bobbie and I can make it happen, so can you. So go out there, chase your dreams, and make your mark on the world.

Bobbie's Encore

Charles didn't mention our most important legacy: our two incredible daughters, out there in the world making a difference. I couldn't be prouder. One's a lawyer, and the other's a doctor, and they're both impacting the lives of so many people.

I have absolutely no regrets about taking a backseat and supporting Charles over the years as we have built our legacy together. It's not a sign of weakness on my part at all. It's about understanding our roles and agreeing to give our best in each of them.

In our family, everyone having a voice is so important. That's why I joined Charles in writing this book. I wanted to shine a light on what it means to stand beside a successful man. It takes sacrifices, and that's okay. I'm proud that we embarked on this journey together and that we're still going strong. Our story isn't over yet.

Your Encore

What hidden desire or dream do you hold within yourself that you have yet to pursue? What steps can you take now to start bringing that dream to life during your own Encore stage?

When reflecting on your life and the impact you want to have, what positive changes or contributions do you aspire to make? How can you align your actions and choices with those aspirations to create a meaningful legacy for others?

ACKNOWLEDGMENTS

As we present *Encore: Embracing Your Retirement Journey* and *Living Your Best Life*, we are deeply grateful to those who generously shared their experiences and insights, enriching this book beyond measure. A special thank you to Robert and Sharon Young, Elaine Vong and Gregory Salton, and Rod Rodriguez, whose personal stories and wisdom have been instrumental in shaping the narrative of this book. Their contributions have not only made the book better but have also provided invaluable perspectives on preparing for, embracing, and enjoying the retirement journey.

This work reflects the author's present recollections of his experiences over time. Occasionally, dialogue consistent with the character or nature of the person speaking has been supplemented. Some names and characteristics have been changed out of a respect for privacy, and some events have been abridged. Names, characters, places, and incidents are based on the author's memories, where others may have conflicting memories. The intent of this work is to encourage the reader to move forward in their career and life, no matter the adversity or obstacles that come their way.

NOTES

Chapter Three

1. Shidler, Lisa. 2008. "Women fear retirement more than men." Investment New. Accessed June 8, 2023. https://www.investmentnews.com/women-fear-retirement-more-than-men-16843
2. Brooks, Rodney. 2020. "The Retirement Crisis Facing Black Americans." US News. Accessed June 8. 2023. https://money.usnews.com/money/retirement/aging/articles/the-retirement-crisis-facing-black-americans
3. Wang, Hansi Lo. 2014. "Latinos Live Longer But Struggle To Save Enough For Retirement." Npr.org. Accessed June 8, 2023. https://www.npr.org/sections/codeswitch/2014/03/27/294880072/latinos-live-longer-but-struggle-to-save-enough-for-retirement
4. Godbout, Ted. 2018. "Asian Americans Appear More Cautious with Retirement Risks, Study Finds." Napa-net.org. Accessed June 8, 2023. https://www.napa-net.org/news-info/daily-news/asian-americans-appear-more-cautious-retirement-risks-study-finds
5. Shidler. "Women fear retirement."
6. King, Brittany. 2022. Those Who Married Once More Likely Than Others to Have Retirement Savings. United States Consensus Bureau. Accessed June 8, 2023. https://www.census.gov/library/stories/2022/01/women-more-likely-than-men-to-have-no-retirement-savings.html

Chapter Five

1. Terrel, Kenneth. 2018. "Age Discrimination Common in Workplace, Survey Says." Aarp.org/ Accessed July 4, 2023.https://www.aarp.org/work/age-discrimination/common-at-work/

2. EEOC. 2022. "Charge Statistics (Charges filed with EEOC) FY 1997 through FY 2022." Eeoc.gov. Accessed July 4, 2023. https://www.eeoc.gov/data/charge-statistics-charges-filed-eeoc-fy-1997-through-fy-2022
3. Neumar, David, Burn, Ian & Button, Patrick. 2017. "Is It Harder for Older Workers to Find Jobs? New and Improved Evidence from a Field Experiment." National Bureau of Economic Research. Accessed July 4, 2023. https://www.nber.org/system/files/working_papers/w21669/w21669.pdf

www.ingramcontent.com/pod-product-compliance
Lightning Source LLC
Chambersburg PA
CBHW070927120626
46546CB00004B/1371

* 9 7 8 1 9 5 4 5 2 1 2 4 7 *